The Schoolchildren's Blizzard

by Marty Rhodes Figley
illustrations by Shelly O. Haas

On My Own
HISTORY

M Millbrook Press/Minneapolis

This book is available in two editions:
Library binding by Millbrook Press, a division of Lerner Publishing Group, Inc.
Soft cover by First Avenue Editions, an imprint of Lerner Publishing Group, Inc.
241 First Avenue North
Minneapolis, MN 55401 U.S.A.

For reading levels and more information, look up this title at
www.lernerbooks.com.

Library of Congress Cataloging-in-Publication Data

Figley, Marty Rhodes, 1948–
    The schoolchildren's blizzard / by Marty Rhodes Figley; illustrations by Shelly O. Haas.
        p.   cm. — (On my own history)
    Summary: In 1888, Sarah, her younger sister Annie, and their classmates survive a
sudden Nebraska blizzard because of the actions of their schoolteacher. Based on the
true story of schoolteacher Minnie Freeman.
    ISBN 978-1–57505–586–2 (lib. bdg. : alk. paper)
    ISBN 978-1–57505–619–7 (pbk. : alk. paper)
    ISBN 978-1–57505–774–3 (eBook)
    [1. Blizzards—Fiction. 2. Sisters—Fiction. 3. Teachers—Fiction. 4. Nebraska—
History—19th century—Fiction.] I. Haas, Shelly O., ill. II. Title. III. Series.
PZ7.F487Sc 2004
    [E]—dc21   2003000157

Manufactured in the United States of America
8 – PP – 9/1/13

With love, for Ben, who is brave in any storm
—M. R. F.

*To the students of Harrington School, with special thanks to
LaMar L., Linda C., and Linda K. for their interest and help*
—S. O. H.

Central Nebraska
January 12, 1888

Sometimes little sisters are trouble,
thought Sarah.
Like this morning.
Sarah and her sister had walked
halfway to school.
Then Annie said,
"I forgot my lunch pail."

"Why don't I share my lunch
with you?" asked Sarah.

"No, I want my own,"
said Annie. "It's special."

Annie had just turned seven yesterday.
This morning, Ma had packed their
lunch pails with fried-egg sandwiches
and leftover birthday cake.
Usually, they had mushy
stewed prunes for dessert.

"If we go back, we'll be late
for school," said Sarah.
"We don't want to disappoint our teacher.
You know what Miss Freeman
always says.
The early bird gets the worm."

"I don't care," said Annie.
"I want my cake."

Sarah and Annie's gingham skirts
flapped against their legs
as they ran back home.
It was more than a mile
across the flat Nebraska prairie.

"At least you forgot your lunch
on a nice day," Sarah said.
"It's not supposed to be
so warm in January."

At the farm, Ma was outside
hanging laundry on the line to dry.
"I thought you might come back
for that cake," she said, laughing.

She handed Annie her lunch pail
and shooed them away.
"Go on, now.
Don't be late for school."

The girls ran all the way to school.

They were just in time.

Their teacher, Miss Minnie Freeman,

stood in the doorway.

She was ringing the school bell.

Miss Freeman nodded hello.

"I was wondering if you
were coming," she said.
Annie told her about
the forgotten lunch.
Miss Freeman smiled.
"That's all right. Go inside, girls."

Miss Freeman was very kind,

Sarah thought.

And she knew so many things.

She could spell any word

and add 10 numbers in her head.

Maybe Sarah could be a teacher someday

if she studied hard.

She would pile her long hair

on top of her head.

She would talk in a soft voice.

She would always be on time,

just like Miss Freeman.

Midvale School had only one room.

Few trees grew on the prairie.

So the school wasn't made of wood.

Instead, large blocks of sod

had been stacked

to build the walls.

Sod was cut from grassy ground.

Thick grass roots held

the dirt together.

Inside the school, the walls and floor
looked like packed dirt.
But Sarah thought the room
was cozy and cheerful.
Miss Freeman had hung calico
curtains at the windows.
She had braided a rag rug
to cover the floor
in front of the coal stove.

Sixteen students went to Midvale School.

Little Rachel, the youngest,

was just 6 years old.

Jake and Seth, the oldest, were 15.

Sarah was in the middle.

She was 9.

That morning, the students studied
the names of the states.
They worked on reading
and spelling.
They practiced writing
on their slates.

At lunchtime, Miss Freeman said,

"It feels like spring.

Let's take our lunches outdoors."

As usual, Annie was a pest.

She tried to eat Sarah's piece of cake.

"You can't have it," said Sarah.

"It was my birthday, not yours,"
said Annie, frowning.
Then she added,
"If there's any cake left
when we get home,
it's going to be all mine."
"We'll see about that," said Sarah.

At recess,

Sarah joined the other children

to play Duck, Duck, Goose.

"I want to play," said Annie.

When it was her turn,

Annie didn't say,

"Duck, Duck, Goose."

She just said "Duck"

over and over again.

Some of the girls giggled.

"You're not playing right,"

Sarah told her.

Annie started to pout.

"You don't like to play with

me because I'm little,"

she whispered.

"That's not true," said Sarah.

"You just need to follow the rules."

Annie turned away.

She looked across the prairie.

Suddenly, she grabbed Sarah's arm.

Sarah followed Annie's gaze.

Her heart started to race

like a frightened prairie rabbit.

The sky didn't look right.

It looked like the clouds
had dropped to the ground.
They were rolling across the prairie
toward the school.
And they were moving fast.
The wind turned cold.
It began to roar like a freight train.

"Get inside!" yelled Sarah.

She pulled Annie toward the schoolhouse.

Miss Freeman rang the bell

with all her might.

"Come, children. Quickly!"

When the children were all safe inside,

Miss Freeman slammed the door.

She fastened it tight.

The students huddled by the stove.
The room was getting
colder every minute.
Sarah began to shiver.
Everyone looked frightened,
even Jake and Seth.
Sarah had never seen them
scared of anything.

"We have plenty of coal
for the stove to keep us warm,"
said Miss Freeman.
"We'll be fine until
the storm ends."
Sarah rubbed her icy hands together.
She hoped her teacher was right.
The wind howled like
a pack of wolves.
The windows started to rattle.
CRASH!
The door burst open.
Swirling snow blew
into the school.
Miss Freeman tried to
push the door shut.
The wind had broken
its leather hinges.

Jake and Seth fixed the hinges,
but the door blew open again.
Rachel started to cry.
The boys found a hammer
and nailed the door shut.

Sarah hoped the nails would hold.

Annie nestled against her.

"It's going to be all right,"

Sarah said.

She stroked Annie's hair.

Then part of the roof
blew off the schoolhouse.
Snow came tumbling down
on the children and the coal stove.
Sarah tried not to cry.
The school was wrecked!
It was no longer a safe place.

If they stayed there,
they might freeze to death.
If they left, they might get lost
in the blizzard.
They might be buried
by the deep snow.
What would they do?

Miss Freeman was yelling.
Sarah could barely hear her
above the roaring wind.
"We'll walk to my house,"
said Miss Freeman.
"It's only half a mile away."
"I can't," said Annie, sobbing.
"I'm cold. I want Ma.
I want to go home!"

Sarah felt the same way.

Then she looked at her teacher.

Miss Freeman looked back calmly
into Sarah's eyes.

Sarah tried to smile.

She would be brave,

just like Miss Freeman.

Miss Freeman lined up the children.

She tied them all to a long rope.

Sarah made sure

she was next to Annie.

"We can do this, children,"

Miss Freeman said.

"The rope will keep us together.

I'll lead the way."

They climbed through the window
and stepped into the knee-deep snow.
Jake stayed at the back
to help Annie and Rachel.
Miss Freeman yelled,
"Don't be afraid. Follow me!"

The blizzard surrounded Sarah
like a whistling white wall.
She staggered blindly through the drifts.
Her eyelids felt like
they were freezing shut.

She held on tightly
to the stiff, frozen rope.
"Are you there, Annie?" she called.
"I'm still here!"
Annie was right behind Sarah.
But her voice sounded far away.

A thousand icy needles
blew against Sarah's face.
She trudged on.
The snow was almost up to her waist.
"Keep going, children,"
Miss Freeman shouted.
"One step at a time!"

It seemed like hours went by.
The cold wind yanked the breath
right out of Sarah's throat.
The snow piled higher and higher.
Surely they had walked
half a mile already.

Sarah's feet felt like two ice blocks.

Her legs tangled together

in her skirt.

She stumbled and fell

in the snow.

She was so tired.

Maybe she could rest

for just a while.

"Get up!" someone yelled.

"We don't want to go too slow!

The early bird gets the worm."

It was Annie.

Her small hands

helped pull Sarah up.

Then Annie pushed her ahead.

Sarah felt tears freeze

on her cheeks.

Annie wouldn't let her quit.

At last, they reached
Miss Freeman's house.
Sarah and Annie stumbled
into the parlor
with the other children.
A toasty fire warmed the room.

"I'm so proud of you,"
said Miss Freeman.
She hugged each child,
even Jake and Seth.
Sarah knew that they were all safe
because of Miss Freeman.

Later that evening,
the blizzard ended.
It was too dark to go home
in the deep snow.
Sarah and Annie rested
on the sofa in front of
Miss Freeman's fireplace.
Wrapped in blankets,
they sipped warm milk.
Miss Freeman said that
tomorrow morning,
Ma and Pa would be able
to bring the wagon.
Then they could go home.
Annie whispered,
"I hope Ma saved some
birthday cake for us."
Sarah hugged her.

"You were so brave today, Annie.

If there's any cake left,

it's all yours.

You deserve it."

Afterword

Sarah and Annie were not real children. But it is true that on January 12, 1888, a deadly storm blew across the central United States. Prairie families didn't have radios or telephones to warn each other of the danger. In Nebraska, the storm was called the Schoolchildren's Blizzard because many children died on their way home from school.

Minnie Freeman's story is also true. She was 19 years old when she led her students to safety from the Midvale School. Newspaper reporters across the country wrote about her bravery. She received more than 80 marriage proposals. A song was written in her honor.

Nebraskans never forgot the Schoolchildren's Blizzard. Some of the survivors formed a club. The Blizzard Club published a book called *In All Its Fury* to share their memories of one of the most dangerous storms in American history.